The Tale of
John Barleycorn

THE TALE OF JOHN BARLEYCORN

or From Barley to Beer

A traditional English ballad

illustrated with woodcuts by

MARY AZARIAN

David R. Godine · Publisher · Boston

First published in 1982 by
David R. Godine, Publisher, Inc.
Post Office Box 450
Jaffrey, New Hampshire 03452

Copyright © 1982 by Mary Azarian

Library of Congress Cataloging in Publication Data

Azarian, Mary.
John Barleycorn, or, From barley to beer.

Summary: A retelling of the traditional
English tale of how barley is turned into beer.
[1. Folklore—England. 2. Beer—Fiction.]
I. Title . II. Title: John Barleycorn
PZ8.1.A93Jo   389.2'6'0942   8203130
ISBN 978-1-56792-604-0   AACR2

FIRST COLOR EDITION, 2018
Printed in China

The calligraphy is by George Laws.

A Note on the Text

The Tale of John Barleycorn is a medieval English ballad celebrating beermaking, one of the oldest arts. Even the ancient Greeks and Romans grew grain and made a kind of beer from it, and the custom has persisted in an unbroken tradition to the present day.

During the middle ages, barley, often known simply as "corn," was the principal grain used both for breadmaking and beermaking. Medieval people regarded beer, like bread, as a food – even a nutritional necessity – and great care was taken in the growth and harvest of the barley crop. The year began with tilling the soil and sowing the seed stored from the previous season's harvest. The crop was carefully watched, and when it reached the proper stage (silvery golden with its characteristic long "beard") the mowers went into the field to begin the harvest. In medieval times, grain was harvested with a short sickle, leaving a considerable amount of stem standing, which was later used for bedding or fodder.

The harvested grain was gathered into sheaves, and the last patch cut was woven into a special figure, called a corn doll, thought to capture the spirit of the grain. The doll was carried with much ceremony to the home of the farmer and kept in a place of honor over the mantle. The following spring it would scattered over the fields to insure a good harvest.

The bundles of grain were stored either in a barn or in thatched mows in the field. Thatching was an art requiring considerable skill, and each thatcher took great pride in creating a mow that would shed water and "stand the storms." Often the thatcher would top his mows with a corn ornament of his own design, which would proclaim the mow as his work.

In fall or winter, when other farm work was less pressing, the barley would be threshed with wooden flails to separate the grain from the stalks. The grain would then be winnowed, allowing the wind to carry away the chaff. The crucial step of malting followed: the grain was watered and allowed to sprout. At a certain point the sprouting was stopped by toasting the grain in an oven. This would convert the starch in the grain to sugar. It took years of practice to determine the proper temperatures required to sprout the grain and roast the malt.

After malting, the grain was carried to the miller who ground it into the meal from which the beer was brewed. In the middle ages, women were the principal brewers. Spring water was added to the ground grain to make a mash, and yeast was introduced to begin the fermentation. Each household brewed on a regular basis, and enormous quantities were made. One fifteenth-century account states that a single household produced over two hundred gallons of beer and ale a month. The modern palate requires the addition of hops for the characteristic flavor of beer, but the medieval drinker was not familiar with hop-flavored brews, although various herbs were often added to enhance the taste and preserve the product. In present-day England, many rural inns and pubs still brew their own beers and ales, each producing a unique product.

Fortunately, it is possible, and fun, to make beer at home. It is doubtful that anyone would consider growing a field of barley, malting it, and using the resultant product to brew beer. Malted syrups, light or dark, are available and, with addition of sugar, hops, and yeast, make a quite acceptable beer. Here is a simple method for making home brew.

Utensils

Five-gallon plastic container, preferably
  made of "food grade" plastic
Piece of clear plastic
  (storm window kits work well)
Stout twine and rubber band
Siphon hose
Bottle capper and caps
Clean reusable beer or soda bottles

Ingredients

One can malt syrup, hopped or plain
Two pounds sugar
Packet of hops (if using plain malt)
Packet of dry yeast, beer or
  ale yeast preferred

Method

Heat four and one-half gallons of pure water to the boil and dissolve the malt syrup and sugar. Add the hops, stir well, and allow to cool to approximately seventy-five degrees. Add the packet of yeast, stir well, and cover loosely with the plastic. Allow the mixture to ferment vigorously for three to four days. When the fermentation begins to subside, tie the plastic very firmly around the brewing vessel with the string and rubber band. This will allow the gases to escape from the brew (or wort), while preventing air from reaching it. After all activity ceases, and the beer begins to clear, it is time to bottle. Using a clean siphon hose tied to a stick, fill clean bottles to within one-half inch of the top.

"Prime" each sixteen-ounce bottle with a scant one-half teaspoon of sugar to achieve carbonation. Cap the bottles and store in a cool place for a month, at which time the brew may be sampled. Brew as often as is deemed necessary to insure an ample supply and attend to cleanliness at each step of the process to obtain consistently good results.

The art of beer- and ale-making at home can rise to almost endless heights of sophistication. While the above instructions should enable anyone to make a palatable product with a minimum of fuss and equipment, many firms can supply the home brewer with products that will insure superior results. Anyone who becomes intrigued with the process is advised to seek additional information from the many books on the subject of brewing. A great variety of ingredients and devices are available from mail order firms.

MARY AZARIAN
July 1982

The actual ballad of John Barleycorn is still sung in England today, and there are many versions of it. All personify the spirit of the grain as "John Barleycorn" and follow the steps of planting, harvesting, brewing, and celebration. Curiously, none of the ballads mentions malting, which is certainly an essential step in the process. It is somehow comforting to think that making beer in the home is an ancient tradition that has continued in an unbroken line to the present day. It is to be hoped that the singing of the song and the brewing of beer will both survive as homely arts.

The Ballad of John Barleycorn

There were three men came down from Kent to plough for wheat and rye. And
these three men made a sol - emn vow John Bar - ley - corn should die. Then
with a plough they ploughed him up and thus they did de - vise to
bur - y him with - in the earth and swore he would not rise.

There were three men

Came down from Kent

To plough for wheat

And rye

And these three men

Made a solemn vow

John Barleycorn

Should die

And thus they did devise ✢

And swore he would not rise ✢

ith harrows strong
They combèd him
And burst clods upon
His head

nd a joyful banquet
Then was made
When Barleycorn
Was dead

He rested still
Within the earth
Till rain from heaven
Did fall

Then he grew up
In branches green
Which so amazed
Them all

hey let him stand

Till midsummer

Then he grew both pale

And wan

nd little Sir John

Grew with a long beard

And so became

A man

Into the field they hied ✤

And made his wounds full wide ✤

They hired men

With sharp pitchforks

Who pricked him to

The heart

The loader served

Him worse than that

For he bound him to

A cart

They wheelèd him

Around the town

Till they came unto

A barn

And there they made

A solemn mow

Of poor

John Barleycorn

Then next the thatcher

He comes in

With reeds and spars

So sharp

He covers over

John Barleycorn

And he must stand

The storms

They hired two
With holly sticks
To beat on him
At once

They thwackèd so
On Barleycorn
That flesh fell from
His bones

They carted him

To a flour mill

And there they burst

His bones

And the miller swore

To murther him

Betwixt a pair

Of stones

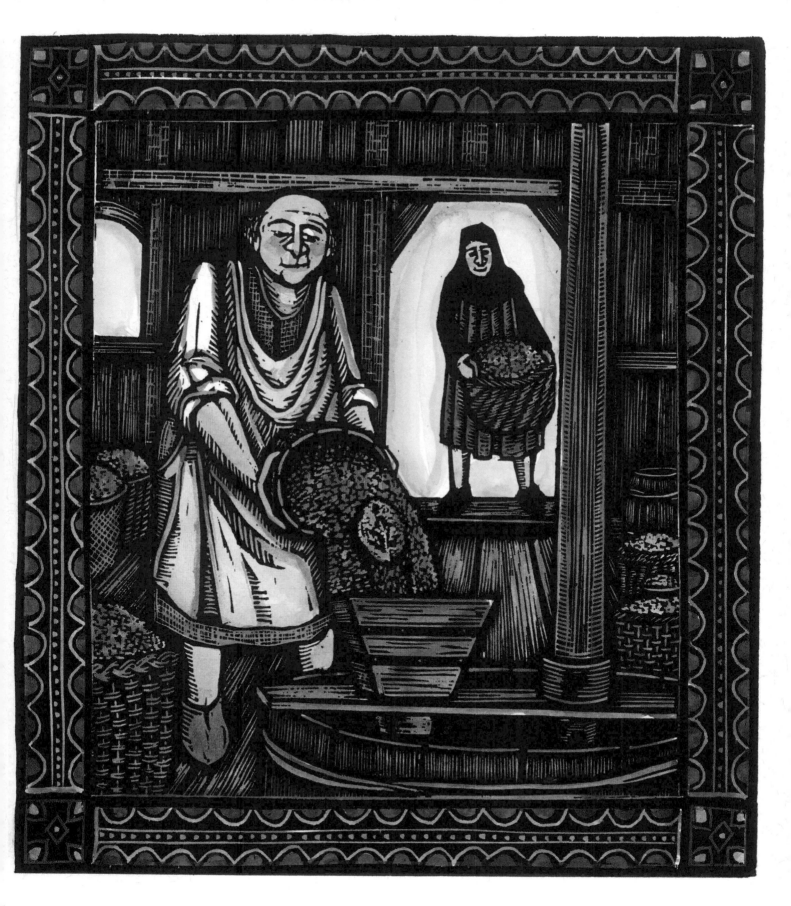

The huntsman he comes out one day ✤

And all the folk did rejoice and sing ✤

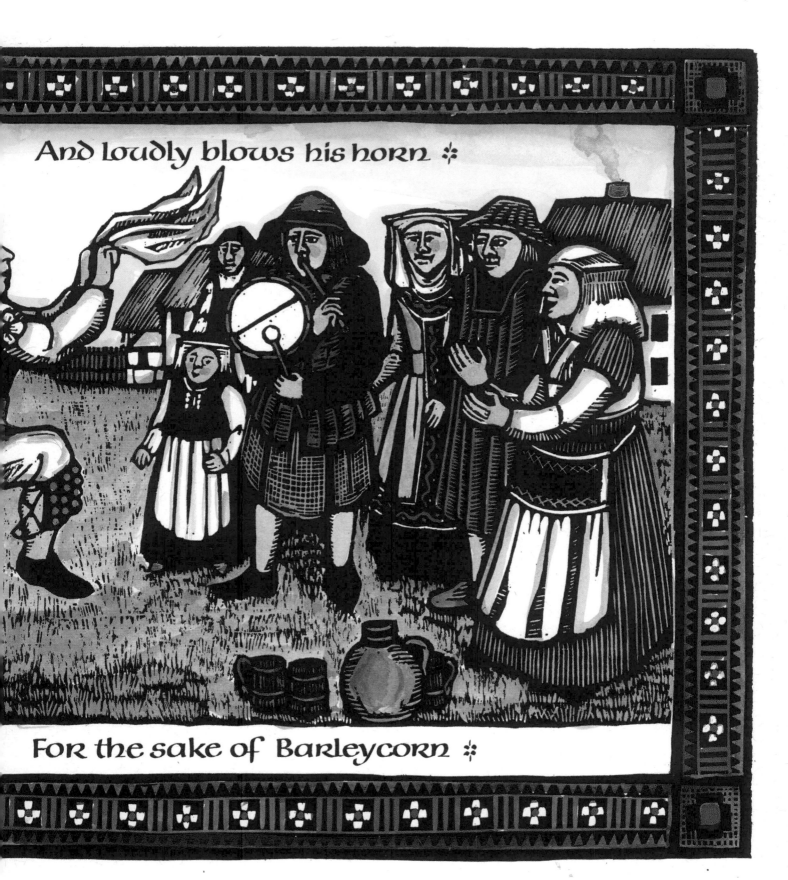

They worked their will

On John Barleycorn

And he lived to tell

The tale

And they pour him from

An earthen jug

And they call him

Homebrewed ale

Barleycorn is the very best seed

That ever was sowed on land

For it would do the heart most good

In the turning of man's hand